History on your Doorstep

Volume 3

Commemorative edition marking the centenary of Bloody Sunday, 21 November 1920

by Liz Gillis and Dublin City Council's Historians in Residence
James Curry, Cormac Moore, Mary Muldowney and
Catherine Scuffil

Edited by Tara Doyle and Cormac Moore

Dublin City Council 2020
Decade of Commemorations Publications Series

First published 2020 by
Dublin City Council
c/o Dublin City Libraries
138-144 Pearse Street
Dublin 2

www.dublincity.ie

Comhairle Cathrach
Bhaile Átha Cliath
Dublin City Council

Designed by Fine Print
Printed by Fine Print

ISBN 978-0-9500512-8-4

Table of Contents

Foreword

So many of us love the history of our local area; we feel connected to the city we live in by reading stories of its past. But history is strewn with bloody battles, massacres and civilian loss-of-life. Sometimes the bloodshed and battles are on our very doorstep and this latest edition in the *History on Your Doorstep* series focuses on a dark day in Dublin city 100 years ago – 21 November 1920, what we now know as Bloody Sunday.

Five historians, including Dublin City Council's team of Historians in Residence, have written this new book, the third in the popular *History on Your Doorstep* series, focusing on the events of and around Bloody Sunday. This special edition marks the centenary of this momentous event in our history, a day which left 32 people dead. Included in the book are chapters on the morning raids on intelligence officers by Michael Collins' Squad, the carnage in Croke Park that afternoon, the reaction of the newspapers, Dick McKee, and the reprisals and attacks on the south side of the city in the days after 21 November 1920.

If your interest is piqued and you would like to read and research more on this topic and indeed on Irish history, there are lists of books at the end of each chapter, many of which can be borrowed for free from your local library.

You can also find the first two volumes of the *History on Your Doorstep* books online at www.dublincity.ie/residential/arts-and-events/decade-commemorations or you can borrow them for free as an ebook from Dublin City Libraries' BorrowBox service.

HAZEL CHU
Lord Mayor of Dublin

About the Authors

JAMES CURRY received his PhD in History & Digital Humanities from NUI Galway in November 2017. He previously graduated with BA and MPhil degrees in history from Trinity College Dublin, where he was awarded the Trinity College Dublin Foundation Scholarship. The author of a book about Dublin cartoonist Ernest Kavanagh plus several co-authored books and articles dealing with modern Irish history, he is the creator of 'Statues of Dublin' channel on YouTube, with associated accounts on Instagram, Twitter and Facebook. James is a former committee member of the Irish Labour History Society and is the Historian in Residence for the North West area of Dublin City.

LIZ GILLIS is an author and historian from the Liberties. She has a degree in Irish History and currently works as a researcher for the *History Show* on RTE Radio. She is the author of six books about the Irish Revolution including, *Women of the Irish Revolution* and *The Hales Brothers and the Irish Revolution* and is co-organiser of the annual conference on the Burning of the Custom House in 1921. In 2018 Liz was a recipient of the Lord Mayor's Award for her contribution to history.

CORMAC MOORE has a PhD in History from De Montfort University in Leicester and an MA in Modern Irish History from UCD. He is Historian in Residence for Dublin North Central and is author of *Birth of the Border: The Impact of Partition in Ireland, The Irish Soccer Split,* and *The GAA V Douglas Hyde: The Removal of Ireland's First President as GAA Patron.* He is a member of the GAA's Decade of Commemorations committee.

MARY MULDOWNEY holds a PhD in History from Trinity College Dublin and also a postgraduate qualification in Adult Continuing Education and Training from the National University of Ireland at Maynooth. She is the Historian in Residence for the Dublin Central area. Mary is the author of books and journal articles, often based on oral history interviews. She is a member of the Grangegorman Histories Working Group and the organising committee of the Irish Labour History Society.

CATHERINE SCUFFIL has an MA in Local History from Maynooth University. She is the Historian in Residence for Dublin South Central and South East. Catherine has written a number of local history books and an abridged version of her MA thesis was awarded the Old Dublin Society's silver medal in 2018.

A team of Historians in Residence work across Dublin City to talk to people about history and promote its sources, especially documents, photos and books in Dublin City Libraries and Archive. The Historians in Residence project is part of Dublin City Council's work under the Decade of Commemorations (1912-22) designation and strives to break down barriers to history. The project is managed by Dublin City Libraries.

Contact them at commemorations@dublincity.ie
 Twitter and Facebook @DubHistorians
www.dublincity.ie/residential/arts-and-events/decade-commemorations

'We have murder by the throat': Bloody Sunday 21 November 1920

Liz Gillis, Historian and Author

As the city of Dublin awoke on Sunday, 21 November 1920, only a select few knew what was going to take place at precisely 9am. Small groups of men, members of the IRA and some members of Cumann na mBan, were walking the deserted streets about to undertake a mission that, if successful, would rock the British intelligence system to its core. As zero hour approached, they waited outside their designated addresses, those inside were completely unaware of what was about to unfold. At 9 o'clock, the sound of church bells ringing could be heard all over the city followed by gunfire. Within ten minutes the operation was over. There was silence, then screams. Fourteen men lay dead, five were wounded, one fatally. 'Bloody Sunday' had dawned.

Why did this event happen and what exactly did happen in those few short minutes? To answer this question, we need to go back to 1918 when Michael Collins was introduced to Eamon Broy, a detective in 'G' Division, the Intelligence Department of the Dublin Metropolitan Police (DMP), stationed in Great Brunswick Street (now Pearse Street) Station. For some time he had been passing intelligence to the Irish Volunteers. Broy told Collins in no uncertain terms, that if the Volunteers were going to wage a war they would not just be taking on the British military but the British intelligence system as well. Those immediately in their sights were the detectives of 'G' Division.

Broy was not the only 'G' man to work with Collins. Others included Joseph Kavanagh, James McNamara and David Neligan. With their help and expertise, Collins began to build his own intelligence organisation.

On Broy's advice, warnings were to be sent to the 'G' men telling them to cease their activities against the Volunteers. Those who listened would come to no harm. *'After all these efforts had been made, a ruthless war was to be made on the hard core that remained'.* That war began in July 1919.

Members of 'G' Division of the Dublin Metropolitan Police. *(1) Nixon (2) Thorton F.*
(3) Wright (4) Gibson (5) Walsh (6) Fennell (7) Dead (8) Williams (9) Whelan Sergt. (10) McKeown
(11) Moncrieff, Bevan (12) O'Neill Sergt. (13) Hall, Richard (14) Healy, Patrick.
(Courtesy of Military Archives, BMH CD/227/35/1)

Michael Collins was now Director of Intelligence for the IRA. He quickly began to expand his organisation, recruiting young men, such as Charles Dalton as his intelligence officers. Other Volunteers were recruited who acted on the information gathered. They were Collins's assassins, 'The Squad'.

Five men from The Squad, left to right Mick McDonnell, Tom Keogh,
Vinny Byrne, Paddy O'Daly and James Slattery
(Courtesy of Kilmainham Gaol Museum/OPW, KMGLM.19PC-1A58-26)

Their first target was Detective Sergeant Patrick Smith, who was shot outside his home in Millmount Avenue, Drumcondra on 30 July 1919. He died some weeks later. This was followed on 12 September by the shooting of Detective Officer Daniel Hoey, yards away from Great Brunswick Street Station.

The British authorities had responded, as was hoped and Dáil Éireann was suppressed and many had to go on the run. 'The Squad' was officially formed.

Over the coming months the assassinations continued, completely undermining the British intelligence system. By the end of the year, 'G' Division was no longer a threat.

Collins's intelligence network continued to grow. Anyone could be an agent and Dublin Castle was caught off guard. Determined to crush Collins and the IRA, things began to change with the appointment in May 1920 of Brigadier-General Sir Ormonde de l'Épéé Winter (known as 'The Holy Terror') as Chief of British Army Intelligence and Deputy Chief of Police in Dublin. Winter was more than up for the challenge of reorganising the British intelligence system. He recruited his own agents; officers who had served abroad in Egypt and Russia. They lived as civilians, as ordinary businessmen in houses around Dublin city. Just as Collins's agents were unknown, so were Winter's men, but not for long.

Brigadier-General Sir Ormonde de l'Épéé Winter
(Courtesy of Kilmainham Gaol Museum/OPW, KMGLM.19PC-1A58-26)

Mrs Caroline Woodcock, whose husband was a lieutenant colonel in the Lancashire Fusiliers, moved to Dublin following her husband's arrival in May 1920. They lived in 28 Upper Pembroke Street with army officers and British agents. In her memoir about Bloody Sunday, she wrote:

> 'Dressed in filthy old clothes and rubber-soled shoes, especially kept for what was frequently very dirty work, they sallied forth in parties of twenty or so, with one or more officers. These raids were usually done at night, and fearful secrecy was observed.

> On these occasions, my husband would come back to our flat about tea-time as usual. He would stay for dinner, and then about 9 o'clock would suddenly announce that he was going out again, and that he would not be back that night.'

Others, like Lieutenant William Lorraine 'Tiny' King were members of 'F' Company Auxiliary Division, based in Dublin Castle. Captain Jocelyn Lee 'Hoppy' Hardy was a member of the Connaught Rangers attached to 'F' Company. These intelligence officers proved to be ruthless in their efforts and were not long in having success against the IRA.

In late 1920 they came close to destroying Collins's entire organisation. Three of his key intelligence staff; Tom Cullen, Liam Tobin and Frank Thornton were arrested. After intense interrogation the men were released, but it was only a matter of time before they struck again. Believing they were gaining the upper hand, Prime Minister David Lloyd George, in his speech at the Lord Mayor's Banquet in London on 9 November stated;

> 'There (Ireland) we have witnessed a spectacle of organised assassination of the most cowardly character… But, at last, unless I am mistaken by the steps we have taken we have murder by the throat.'

Collins realised the net was tightening and he decided to strike. The extent of Collins's network was amazing. Information on the agents and officers came from everywhere. For example, Lily Mernin, 'Lt. G', worked as a typist in Dublin Castle. With a friend, she went to the whist drives in Dublin Castle and talked to the Auxiliaries and officers. She then went for lunch with IRA intelligence officer Frank Saurin and identified those she had met. She got the names and addresses of some of those who were targeted on Bloody Sunday, including that of Lieutenant Henry James Angliss. Through a conversation with a work colleague, Mernin learned that Angliss had been involved in the shooting of Sinn Féin councillor John Lynch in the Exchange Hotel in September. This information sealed his fate.

Mernin was one of many. Molly O'Reilly, who was in Cumann na mBan, worked as a waitress in the Bon Bouche restaurant in Dawson Street, from where she also got names and addresses of British agents. Madge Clifford, Central Branch, Cumann na mBan, pretended to be looking for digs in a quiet part of the city and carried out surveillance of the properties to see who was living there. Intelligence officer Charles Dalton made contact with a young woman named Maudie who worked as a maid in number 28 Upper Pembroke Street. She was suspicious of the residents there and acquired for him the contents of the wastepaper baskets. What he found was alarming. They discovered *torn up documents which referred to the movements of wanted Volunteers and also photographs of wanted men*. Even within their own ranks the British were not safe. John Reynolds, 'F' Company Auxiliaries, regularly gave information about his colleagues. Constable Patrick Mannix, who provided some of the names and addresses of British agents, was one of at least twelve DMP men working for Collins.

With the information gathered, the plans for Bloody Sunday were put in place. Lists were drawn up of potential targets which were then presented to Cathal Brugha who, as Minister for Defence, gave the final sanction. He had at least fifteen names removed from the original list, *'if to his mind there was the slightest loop-hole for uncertainty about an agent or spy, then that individual could not be dealt with.'*

Once the names of the targeted men were confirmed, the date and time was set. On Sunday, 21 November, a Gaelic football match between Dublin and Tipperary was scheduled to take place in Croke Park. Thousands were expected in the city and this would give the perfect cover for the operation that would take place at 9 o'clock that morning. Thirty-five names were on the final list. This was a massive operation, involving over 130 people. Secrecy was of the utmost importance and few were privy to the plans. The night before, specially chosen men from the four Dublin battalions of the IRA were told what they were to do the next morning. Members of Cumann na mBan were also informed that they would be needed for duty. The three Cooney sisters, Annie, Eileen and Lily were told by Christy Byrne, 'C' Company, 4th Battalion to be at mass at University Church on St. Stephen's Green and wait for him and his men to take the guns after the operation.

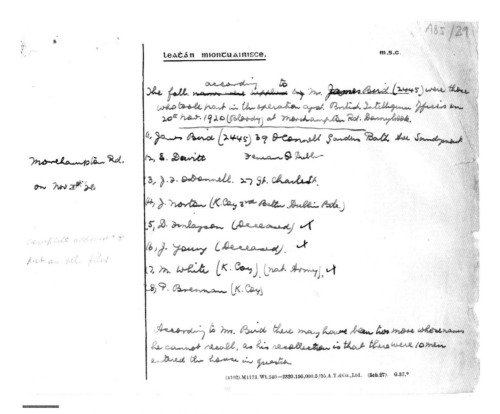

List of some of the men involved in Bloody Sunday
(Courtesy of Military Archives, Brigade Activity Report pg. 29 A85 Dublin
Brigade - General Activities, Military Service Pensions Collection)

That night the IRA was dealt a severe blow. Dublin Brigade officers Dick McKee and Peadar Clancy had met with Collins at Vaughan's Hotel on Parnell Square to go over the plans one last time. McKee and Clancy then made their way to Gloucester Street (now Sean MacDermott Street). Unknown to them they were followed by a military policeman, who alerted Dublin Castle and a raiding party soon arrived at the house of Seán Fitzpatrick where they were staying. The men were arrested and taken to Dublin Castle. Conor Clune, a Gaelic Leaguer from County Clare was also arrested. He was in Vaughan's Hotel when it was raided and had nothing to do with the morning's events.

The next morning, groups of Volunteers made their way to their designated locations. At 9 o'clock, knocks came to the doors of a number of houses on the south side of the city while a party of fifteen men entered the Gresham Hotel on the north side.

At 22 Lower Mount Street Lieutenant Angliss was shot dead. Lieutenant Peel barricaded himself in his room and managed to evade being shot. Two Auxiliary officers, cadets Garniss and Morris were killed whilst returning to Beggars Bush barracks to get reinforcements. At 117 Morehampton Road, Lieutenant MacLean and Thomas Herbert Smith, the landlord, were shot dead. A Mr. Caldow was wounded. At 38 Upper Mount Street, Lieutenants Bennett and Ames were killed. Volunteer Michael J. Lawless recalled what he saw in his witness statement:

> *'I got a glimpse in another room of three men standing up in pyjamas facing the wall with their hands on the wall. I stayed in the hall while the shots were fired in that room.'*

At 28 Upper Pembroke Street, Major Dowling and Captain Price were shot dead; Colonel Woodcock, Captain Keenlyside, Colonel Montgomery and Lieutenant Murray were all wounded. Paddy Flanagan, captain of 'C' Company, 3rd Battalion was in charge of the attacking party. Seventeen-year-old Charles Dalton, GHQ Intelligence, was there to gather up the officers' papers. Remembering the events, he later wrote:

'I accompanied Flanagan and two other Volunteers to a room at the top of the house occupied by two officers, one of these being Lieut. Dowling. We knocked at the door and pushed it open. The two officers were awake in bed. They were told to stand up and were then shot.

We proceeded down the staircase to the hallway, where a number of other officers had been rounded up from their rooms and were lined up against the side of the staircase that led in the direction of the basement. Our reaching this level was the signal for the volley.'

Major Dowling and Captain Price were shot dead in this house at 28 Pembroke Street Upper (Courtesy of Liz Gillis)

ÓGLAIGH NA h-ÉIREANN.

OLD DUBLIN BRIGADE 1916-1923.   2nd Battalion.

75, N.C. Rd.,
DUBLIN, 10/3/1935.

An Rúnaí,
Office of the Referee,
Griffith Barracks.

A Chara,

In reply to a recent inquiry addressed by you to Mr. O.
Traynor, T.D., I give you below the names of the men who were in action
at the Gresham Hotel, on Bloody Sunday, 1920.   The men were all
members of D.Company of 2nd Battalion.

Patrick Moran (Captain) was in charge. He was executed later
at Mountjoy Prison.

Arthur Beasley)
James Foley   )   Officers of the Company.

Michael Noone. (now Commandant of Collins Barracks, Dublin.)

J. Moloney.

W. Hogan.

J. Doyle.

M. Kilkelly.

G. McCann.

R. McGrath.

P. Kennedy.

J. Glynn.

M. Durnan.

Nicholas Leonard.

M. Donelan.

The men carried out the task which was entrusted to them.

Mise, le meas mor,

(SGD)   ? P. Mac Ionnrais
(?)

P.S.
Owing to sickness in my own home and among many of our members
there has been delay in obtaining replies to your inquiries on this
matter and others.

(SGD)   ?

List of men present at the Gresham Hotel (Courtesy of Military
Archives, pg. 19 A85 Dublin Brigade - General Activities)

119 Baggot Street Lower where Captain Baggallay was shot dead
(Courtesy of Liz Gillis)

92 Baggot Street Lower
(Courtesy of Liz Gillis)

Captain Patrick McCormack and Leonard Wilde, a civilian, were killed in the Gresham Hotel. Paddy Moran, 'D' Company, 2nd Battalion was in charge of the group. The men knew exactly where to go, disconnecting the telephone lines before carrying out the shootings. Captain Baggallay was shot dead in 119 Lower Baggot Street. Lieutenant Fitzgerald died at 28 Earlsfort Terrace. At 92 Lower Baggot Street, Captain Newbury was shot dead in front of his wife. According to a Hansard report:

'Captain Newbury and wife together tried to hold the door against them and almost succeeded in shutting it when the men fired through the door wounding Captain Newbury, who though losing blood nevertheless got to the window, flung it open, and was half-way out when the murderers burst into the room. Mrs. Newbury flung herself in their way, but they pushed her aside and fired seven shots into her husband's body. The police found the body half in and half out, covered with a blanket which Mrs. Newbury, though in a prostrate condition, had placed over it.'

Mrs Newbury was heavily pregnant. She died giving birth a few weeks later, her baby died as well. An awful, tragic consequence of the morning's events.

VICTIMS OF "THE MURDER GANG": OFFICERS KILLED IN DUBLIN.

PHOTOGRAPHS BY BENDER AND LEWIS, NEWSPAPER ILLUSTRATIONS, LAFAYETTE, I.B., PARISIAN STUDIOS (GILLINGHAM), PHOTOPRESS, AND VANDYK.

MAJOR C. M. G. DOWLING, GRENADIER GUARDS.

CAPT. W. F. NEWBERRY, 4TH QUEEN'S (ROYAL WEST SURREY) REGIMENT.

CAPTAIN P. McCORMACK, R.A.V.C.

LIEUTENANT D. L. MacLEAN, LATE RIFLE BRIGADE.

CADET FRANK GARNISS.

LIEUT. H. ANGLISS, D.C.M. INNISKILLING FUSILIERS.

LIEUTENANT G. BENNETT, LATE R.A.

CADET C. A. MORRIS, AUXILIARY R.I.C.

CAPTAIN LEONARD PRICE, M.C. LATE MIDDLESEX REGIMENT.

LIEUTENANT A. AMES, LATE GRENADIER GUARDS.

CAPTAIN G. T. BAGGALLAY (EXTRA REGIMENTALLY EMPLOYED).

On the day following the Sinn Fein murders in Dublin (on Sunday, November 21), Sir Hamar Greenwood, Chief Secretary for Ireland, said in the House of Commons : "I hope that this series of cold-blooded and carefully planned atrocities will bring vividly before the House and the public the cruel reality of the Irish situation. We are fighting an organised band of paid assassins, whose plans, recently discovered, include the destruction of life and property in this country as well as in Ireland. . . . Now I shall read the details of, I think, one of the most foul tragedies in the history of our Empire. There have been 14 deaths and 6 injured, including 1 assassin, and 3 assassins captured red-handed with arms." We have not space here to give the details referred to, even in outline, nor have we been able to obtain portraits of all the murdered officers. The list of killed included also Capt. Fitzgerald, Mr. T. H. Smith, and Mr. L. Wilde. In earlier published accounts Lieut. Angliss was mentioned incorrectly as Lieut. Mahon. We have just heard of the mistake, too late to alter it on pages already gone to press.

(Courtesy of *Illustrated London News*)

As quickly as it had begun, the operation was over. In all, fifteen men died as a result of the events that morning, including Colonel Montgomery who later died of his wounds; four were wounded. Volunteer Frank Teeling, 2nd Battalion, Dublin Brigade, IRA was shot in the stomach and was taken into custody. There would have been more casualties had everyone on the list been at their lodgings. One who got away was 'Hoppy' Hardy. When word got out about the shootings, panic set in around the city. Dublin Castle was a hotbed of activity, with officials and their wives all going there for protection.

And what of Michael Collins? Where was he and what was his reaction to the news? Collins was in Devlin's pub in Parnell Street that morning waiting for his aide, Joe O'Reilly to bring word. According to Frank O'Connor, *'When O'Reilly arrived Collins listened, white and defiant, with no expression of pleasure'*.

But someone was going to pay for what had happened that morning and the carnage that followed is described in the next chapters.

In a matter of minutes, British intelligence was dealt a severe blow, it was not destroyed but the IRA had proved that it did not have 'murder by the throat'.

It is best to leave the last word to the man who orchestrated the assassinations that morning and explain why he chose to strike such a blow against the Crown forces.

> *'My one intention was the destruction of the undesirables who continued to make miserable the lives of ordinary decent citizens. I have proof enough to assure myself of the atrocities which this gang of spies and informers have committed. Perjury and torture are words too easily known to them.*
>
> *If I had a second motive it was no more than a feeling such as I would have for a dangerous reptile.*
>
> *By their destruction the very air is made sweeter. That should be the future's judgement on this particular event. For myself, my conscience is clear. There is no crime in detecting and destroying, in war-time, the spy and the informer. I have paid them back in their own coin.'* (Michael Collins 1921).

> *Thanks to Catherine Scuffil, John Healy, Mícheál Ó Doibhilín and Paul O'Brien.*

Further Reading

- Dalton, Charles. *With the Dublin Brigade: Espionage and Assassination with Michael Collins' Intelligence Unit.* Mercier, 2014.

- Hart, Peter (ed.). *Irish Narratives, British Intelligence in Ireland, 1920-21. The Final Reports.* Cork University Press, 2002.

- Hittle, J.B.E. *Britain's Counterinsurgency Failure: Michael Collins and the Anglo-Irish War.* Washington, 2011.

- McMahon, Paul. *British Spies and Irish Rebels: British Intelligence and Ireland 1916-1945.* Boydell Press, 2008.

- O'Connor, Frank. *The Big Fellow.* Poolbeg Press, 1996.

- Price, Dominic. *We Bled Together: Michael Collins, The Squad and the Dublin Brigade.* The Collins Press, 2017.

- Sheehan, William. *British Voices. From the Irish War of Independence 1918-1921: The Words of British Servicemen who Were There.* The Collins Press, 2005.

- Woodcock, Caroline. *An Officer's Wife in Ireland.* Parkgate Publications, 1994. (First published in 1921)

- Bureau of Military History Witness Statements and Military Service Pensions Collection, Military Archives.

Croke Park on Bloody Sunday, 21 November 1920

Cormac Moore, Historian in Residence, Dublin North Central

After fourteen suspected British intelligence personnel were killed, and one fatally injured, by the IRA on the morning of 21 November 1920, the city of Dublin was in a heightened state of frenzy. Fearing that Croke Park could become a target for the British forces, Luke O'Toole, secretary general of the GAA, consulted with GAA officials on whether to go ahead with the scheduled challenge Gaelic football match that afternoon between Dublin and Tipperary.

The match ticket cost 1 shilling
(Courtesy of GAA Museum)

Just before the match was due to start, O'Toole was warned by IRA members that a force of military and Auxiliaries were being mobilised for Croke Park and strongly advised him to call off the match. Fearing that an announcement to clear the stadium would lead to a panic-induced exodus, a compromise was reached and O'Toole agreed to close the turnstiles to try and limit the crowd. O'Toole's instructions went unheeded with people continuing to pour in through the turnstiles. Anywhere up to 15,000 people attended Croke Park that afternoon.

There was good reason to fear that Croke Park would be a target of the British. Although the GAA publicly declared it was a non-political body, it was closely aligned with Sinn Féin and the Irish republican movement.

Luke O'Toole standing between Michael Collins and Harry Boland in September 1921. (Courtesy of GAA Museum)

The match between Dublin and Tipperary was organised by the Volunteers Dependants' Fund Committee for the benefit of the relatives of imprisoned or dead republicans. Dublin Castle compiled lists of Irish organisations it classified as political, with the GAA included as one such organisation.

The evidence available does suggest that the British initially planned to raid Croke Park in an attempt to search for IRA members who were involved in the killings that morning and not as a reprisal mission. The British were correct in speculating that some of those involved in the events of the morning would be at Croke Park. Paddy Moran, who captained the IRA 'D' Company, 2nd Battalion's attack in the Gresham Hotel that killed Patrick McCormack and Leonard Wilde in the morning, was involved in the other match played in Croke Park that Sunday. Dunleary Commercials played Erin's Hope in a replayed Dublin intermediate football final at 11:30am. Moran was secretary of Dunleary Commercials and arrived in time for the team photograph. The goalkeeper of the Dublin team, Johnny McDonnell, was involved in the killings of Peter Ames and George Bennett on Mount Street. Afterwards he took a boat back over the Liffey to join his teammates from O'Toole's GAA club to prepare for the match against Tipperary.

At 1:30pm, the commander of the British Army in Ireland Nevil Macready sent a message to Lieutenant Colonel Robert Bray at Collinstown Aerodrome (present day site of Dublin airport), where the 2nd Battalion, Duke of Wellingtons (West Riding Regiment) was stationed, ordering the battalion to '*surround the ground and picquet all exits...About a quarter of an hour before the match is over a Special Intelligence Officer will warn by megaphone all people present at the match that they will only leave the grounds by the exits. Anybody attempting to get away elsewhere will be shot. All male persons will be stopped, searched*'.

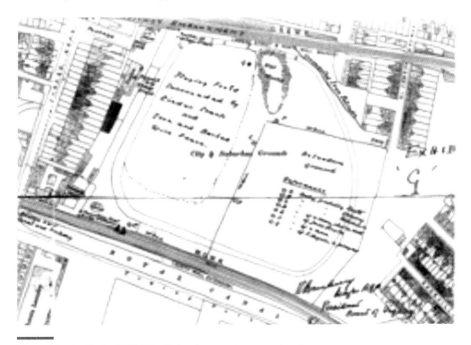

Map of Croke Park, 1920. The Belvedere rugby grounds where so many tried to escape to is on the right. (Courtesy of GAA Museum)

Bray's regiment arrived at different exit points outside Croke Park at 3:15pm. Most of the crowd were oblivious to developments outside as the game was about to start, 30 minutes later than originally planned. The crowd were also distracted by an aeroplane flying overheard, firing a flare as it did so.

While Bray's military battalion waited outside Croke Park, with its mission to block exit points, the Royal Irish Constabulary (RIC), including the Black and Tans and Auxiliaries, were en route. Their orders were to detain and search all the men attending the match. Major Edward Lawrence Mills was in overall command of the mixed police force. Another auxiliary, Major George Dudley was in command of the Black and Tans. At 3:25pm, police cars arrived at the canal bridge along Jones' Road. When the police trucks arrived, the ticket sellers outside the ground fled.

Just 10 minutes after the game had started, the first shots were fired from the canal bridge. 11-year-old William 'Perry' Robinson was perched on a tree watching the match. Hearing the commotion outside, he turned around and a bullet hit him in the chest, exiting through his right shoulder, knocking him from the tree. He was taken to Drumcondra Hospital where he died two days later from his wounds. Perry was from Little Britain Street in Dublin's inner city. Just a month beforehand, on 16 October, Perry's 26-year-old cousin William had been shot dead between Capel and Mary Streets. Whilst Perry was felled with the first bullet, the second or third bullet killed 10-year-old Jerome O'Leary from Blessington Street. O'Leary was sitting on the wall at the southwest end of the field and was shot through the right side of his head.

The combined forces of RIC, Black and Tans and Auxiliaries ran towards the turnstiles at the canal end corner, and ordered a ticket seller named Thomas Doyle to open the gate. As soon as he did, the Black and Tans 'began firing towards the hill on the other side of the ground'.

21-year-old Joe Traynor was shot in the back as he climbed over the canal end wall. He was found by the Ring family of Sackville Gardens who took him to their house and tried to help him but he was bleeding heavily. The Rings carried him to a laneway on Sackville Avenue where an ambulance took him to Jervis Street Hospital but he didn't survive. From Ballymount, Traynor was a talented Gaelic footballer who was captain of the Young Emmets team in Inchicore.

The Black and Tans started firing into the ground from the bridge looking into Croke Park. Panic ensued with people running onto the pitch, trying to escape the shooting. In the corner of the ground near Luke O'Toole's house, 30-year-old Michael Feery tried to pull himself over the top of the wall but his thigh became impaled on a spike and he later bled to death in a house on Russell Street. Feery, a former First World War soldier, lived in Gardiner Place with his wife and son. By 1920 he was unemployed and reliant on odd jobs to make money.

The indiscriminate firing continued. A ricochet bullet hit 14-year-old John William 'Billy' Scott in the chest. His wounds were so bad that people later thought he had been bayoneted. After he was shot he was taken to a house on St. James' Avenue but died there shortly after. The Scott family resided close to Croke Park on Fitzroy Avenue.

The panicked crowd tried to escape from Croke Park but were pushed back by the RIC and Auxiliaries. Those who escaped onto St. James' Avenue came under machine-gun fire and returned to the ground. Exit gates were clogged near Hill 60 and one of the gates was flattened. Many people hid in nearby houses. A stampede developed which resulted in two people being crushed to death, James Teehan and James Burke. 26-year-old Teehan, originally from Tipperary, had a pub with his brother John on Green Street in the tenements of the Ormond slum near Sackville Street. 44-year-old James Burke was from Windy Arbour in Dublin and worked for Terenure Laundry. He was married with five children.

To try to escape the carnage, hundreds risked the twenty-foot drop over the wall into the Belvedere rugby grounds beside Croke Park. Patrick O'Dowd was shot in the head as he was helping someone over the wall to Belvederes. At 57 years of age, O'Dowd was the oldest victim that afternoon. He lived with his wife and two children on Lower Buckingham Street and worked as a labourer with Clarke's Builders in Fairview.

48-year-old James Mathews also attempted to escape Croke Park via the Belvedere grounds. His body was later found near the wall separating Croke Park from Belvederes with a bullet wound in his leg. Mathews was a labourer who lived on North Cumberland Street.

Jane Boyle and her fiancé Daniel Byron were caught in the crush heaving towards the exit. 28-year-old Jane was killed, shot in the back and crushed by the crowd. She was from Lennox Street in Portobello and worked in Olhausen's butchers on Talbot Street. Jane and Daniel were due to be married the Friday after the match but instead she was buried in her wedding dress.

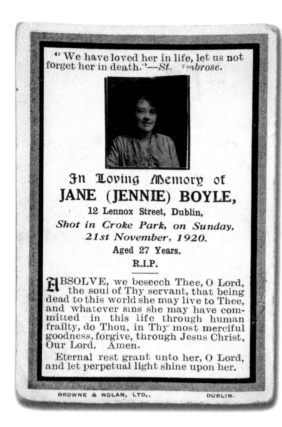

"We have loved her in life, let us not forget her in death."—*St. Ambrose.*

In Loving Memory of
JANE (JENNIE) BOYLE,
12 Lennox Street, Dublin,
Shot in Croke Park, on Sunday,
21st November, 1920.
Aged 27 Years.
R.I.P.

ABSOLVE, we beseech Thee, O Lord, the soul of Thy servant, that being dead to this world she may live to Thee, and whatever sins she may have committed in this life through human frailty, do Thou, in Thy most merciful goodness, forgive, through Jesus Christ, Our Lord. Amen.
Eternal rest grant unto her, O Lord, and let perpetual light shine upon her.

BROWNE & NOLAN, LTD., DUBLIN.

Memorial card for Jane Boyle. Jane became separated from her fiancé as they fled Croke Park, she was shot in the back and crushed in the crowd (Courtesy of GAA Museum)

When the shooting started, most of the players from Dublin and Tipperary dropped to the ground to escape the bullets. Tipperary corner-back Michael Hogan lay flat on the ground and wriggled his way off the pitch but was shot in the back and died shortly afterwards. He was 24-years-of-age. Hogan was the only player to be killed on Bloody Sunday. He was a farmer from Grangemockler in County Tipperary and a member of the IRA. Hogan Stand at Croke Park was named in his honour in 1926.

Michael Hogan was shot dead in Croke Park as he tried to get off the pitch. He was a corner-back on the Tipperary team on Bloody Sunday (Courtesy of GAA Museum)

As Hogan lay dying, Thomas Ryan said a prayer into his ear. A bullet hit Ryan. He tried to struggle off the pitch. He was taken to Jervis Street Hospital where he later died. 27-year-old Ryan was originally from Glenbrien in County Wexford and lived with his wife and two children in Arbour Hill. He also was a member of the IRA, who, in the morning was sent to Marlborough Road on the lookout for a British spy. The spy was not there though and Ryan took no further part in the events that morning.

Daniel Carroll was on Russell Street on his way home when he got struck by a bullet in his thighbone. Carroll, who was 30 years of age, was admitted to Jervis Street Hospital where he died from his wounds two days later. Originally from Templederry in Tipperary, he managed Martin Kennedy's pub in Drumcondra.

The last person to die from the attack in Croke Park was 19-year-old Tom Hogan. Hogan was shot in the shoulder and admitted to the Mater Hospital but the wound was so bad that his right arm had to be amputated. After the operation, gas gangrene set in and he died five days later. Originally from Kilmallock in Limerick, Hogan joined the IRA when he moved to Dublin. He lived at St James' Terrace in Dolphin's Barn where he worked as a mechanic.

The fourteenth and last Croke Park victim of Bloody Sunday, Tom Hogan died in the Mater Hospital on 26 November 1920 (Courtesy of Mercier Archive)

In just 90 seconds of shooting, 14 people were dead or dying, with many more wounded. In just 90 seconds, the police fired 114 rounds of rifle ammunition and an unknown amount of revolver ammunition. In just 90 seconds, Croke Park was transformed from a place of play to a place of pathos.

Both Mills and Dudley ordered the shooting to stop. There were long queues of people, hands in the air, waiting to be searched and the ground was shot to pieces. 'Apples and oranges were strewn everywhere. Umbrellas and hats covered the field.' Priests gave the last rites to the wounded and dying.

Croke Park the day after the horror of Bloody Sunday (Courtesy of GAA Museum)

The truth of what actually happened was immediately contested and muddied. The House of Commons debated the events the following day. The Chief Secretary for Ireland Hamar Greenwood gave accounts of the killings from Sunday morning, going into detail on how each person was killed, but did not mention the events in Croke Park in the afternoon. The House was in a frenzy and when Joe Devlin, Irish nationalist MP for West Belfast, tried to ask Greenwood to comment on the killings in Croke Park, he was continuously shouted at and told to sit down. Some from the government benches even chanted, 'Kill Him!'. Refusing to relent, Devlin's legs were grabbed by a government backbencher Major Molson who pulled Devlin down. The speaker was forced to suspend the sitting.

A day later, Greenwood gave the fullest official explanation for the events in Croke Park, claiming the police were fired upon first and that about 30 revolvers thrown away were picked up on the ground. He concluded by saying, 'These casualties include perfectly innocent persons whose death I deeply regret. The responsibility for them, however, rests entirely upon those assassins whose existence is a constant menace to all law-abiding persons in Ireland'.

Two courts of military inquiry were held in the immediate aftermath of the shootings in Jervis Street and Mater Hospitals. The outcomes of the inquiries and the testimony of Major Mills were buried for 80 years. Whilst the Mater Hospital Court contended that the police were fired on initially, it also concluded that the 'fire of the RIC was carried out without orders and exceeded the demands of the situation'.

Both inquiries heard evidence from about 30 people, a mixture of civilian and crown witnesses. While many of the crown witnesses claimed they were fired on first, civilian witnesses, including Luke O'Toole from the GAA, said the first shots came from the police on the canal bridge. The claims by crown witnesses that there were armed IRA pickets outside the ground were countered by civilian witnesses that those alleged pickets were ticket sellers. There also were inconsistencies in the evidence from crown witnesses, with some claiming they were shot at first, and others who were right beside them, claiming they were not.

Perhaps the most damning evidence of all was that of Major Mills, the person in charge of the combined police forces at Croke Park that day. In his report, he appears to corroborate eyewitness accounts, claiming 'as no shots were coming from the football field and all the RIC constables seemed excited and out of hand, I rushed along and stopped the firing with the assistance of Major Fillery who was in the car with me'. He also contradicted the official version that arms had been found left behind in Croke Park, stating 'We found no arms on any of the people attending the match…When the ground was cleared we searched for arms and found none'.

The most likely explanation of what happened in Croke Park on Sunday 21 November 1920 is that the initial intention by the military and police leaders was to carry out a search operation but their forces had other ideas and sought revenge for what had happened to their colleagues in the morning. E.C. Barton, a British soldier who was stationed in Dublin on Bloody Sunday wrote an autobiography in 1976 where he recalled that day's events. Throughout that day he was getting scraps of information on what happened in the morning. There were even rumours that some of the officers had been killed with coal hammers. Barton claims that the troops were so enraged, they 'were burning to get out and take affairs into their own hands'. In fact, the men of one regiment intended to march out of their barracks but were 'stopped just in time. At that time all barrack gates were locked and a quarter guard mounted'. Whatever intentions the leaders had, it was clear many of the Crown forces were hell bent on revenge and their actions in Croke Park were almost certainly acts of reprisal. The massacre in Croke Park was yet another example, the most notorious one, of the British taking revenge on civilians for IRA attacks on its forces. When conflated with another similar massacre in Amritzar in India in 1919 when hundreds of civilians were killed by British troops, Bloody Sunday further damaged Britain's international reputation. Britain was losing the propaganda war with Sinn Féin.

Bloody Sunday transformed Croke Park from not just a playing field but now a martyred ground. It also served to elevate and overstate the role the GAA played in the revolutionary movement. While Bloody Sunday has never been forgotten, nor has one of the victims that day, Tipperary footballer Michael Hogan, the other victims were largely neglected for years. Eight of the fourteen dead were in unmarked graves until 2015. The GAA established a Bloody Sunday Graves Project, in tandem with the families, to mark each grave plot with a headstone. Now, finally the people most affected by that afternoon's events are coming to the forefront in remembrance, the fourteen people who so needlessly lost their lives because of their presence at a match in Croke Park.

Dublin Team on 21 November 1920
(Courtesy of GAA Museum)

Further Reading

- Barton, E.C. *Let the Boy Win His Spurs.* The Research Publishing Co., 1976.

- Carey, Tim and de Búrca, Marcus. *Bloody Sunday 1920: New Evidence.* History Ireland, 2003.

- Foley, Michael. *The Bloodied Field: Croke Park. Sunday 21 November 1920.* O'Brien Press, 2nd Revised Edition 2020.

- Leeson, David. *Death in the Afternoon.* Canadian Journal of History, 2003.

- Ó Tuathaigh, Gearóid (ed.). *The GAA & Revolution in Ireland 1913-1923.* The Collins Press, 2015.

- Bureau of Military History Witness Statements, Military Archives.

- The Dublin Castle Records 1798-1926.

DUBLIN'S WEEK-END OF TRAGEDY. APPALLING SCENES.

In the course of yesterday's shooting tragedy at Croke Park a large number of persons were killed and injured. The photographs show some of the wounded who arrived at Jervis St. Hospital, assisted by their friends—(left to right) Mr. J. Fagan, Denmark Row, ex-soldier, shot in the leg; Mr. T. Maher, Drumcondra, wounded in the knee, and Master P. Caulfield, Corporation St., received a bullet in the wrist.

"Irish Independent" Photos

Michael Curley, 4 Emerald place, who was wounded in the shoulder, leaving Jervis St. after his injuries were attended to.

Play had been in progress only a short period when the forces of the Crown arrived. The photograph shows the start of the unfinished match.

The funeral took place in London of Constable. O. Buntrock, R.I.C., who was killed during the week. The photograph shows the coffin being carried to the grave by members of the R.I.C.

Topical.

A smoke screen was put up in Stephen's Green, Dublin, whilst the Auxiliary Cadets of the R.I.C. were making a raid.

Topical.

Mr. Richard W. Beamish.

Miss Stella Johnson.

Over 300 men recruited for the Special Constabulary on arrival at Newtownards were played by the R.I.C. band to the depot.

Topical.

Bloody Sunday 1920 in the Press

Mary Muldowney, Historian in Residence, Central Area

During the War of Independence, newspapers were subject to the censorship provisions of the Defence of the Realm Act (DORA), which had been introduced on 8 August 1914 at the outbreak of the First World War, 'for securing public safety'. Its use by the British administration in Ireland became significantly more oppressive after the 1916 Easter Rising. Newspapers were subject to the control of the military authorities, leading to a certain amount of self-censorship in the nationalist press to avoid suppression. Nevertheless, there was also a great deal of criticism of the Dublin Castle administration and increasingly sympathetic coverage of Sinn Féin activities. This chapter will focus on the press reaction in Ireland in the immediate aftermath of Bloody Sunday.

It can be quite strange to modern sensibilities to see the front pages of newspapers in the 1920s carrying a range of small ads and public notices rather than featuring the dramatic headlines we would see today if the horrific events of 21 November 1920 were to happen now. On Monday, 22 November the *Irish Independent* did not mention the previous day's events until page three, in a newspaper that typically of the time, was only eight pages long.

The coverage featured some photographs of casualties and the beginning of the match at Croke Park, on the same page as pictures of police funerals, of victims of shootings in Cork, the announcement of an engagement to be married and the laying of the foundation stone of a new parish church at Finglas by the Archbishop of Dublin. There was also a picture of Art O'Brien, with a caption identifying him as the President of the Irish Self-Determination League, who had received a threatening letter signed "Black and Tan". It seems like a peculiar editorial decision not to position the pictures from Bloody Sunday with the reporting of the day's terrible events but it was probably because of technical restrictions in the printing presses of the day and before news photography became an important element of journalism.

The *Irish Independent's* editorial approach to the story, as evidenced by pages four and five of the paper, seems to have been to balance the coverage of the shootings by the Squad in the morning of 21 November with equal attention to the reprisals in Croke Park in the afternoon. This was a major change from the stance taken by the paper after the 1916 Rising, when editor Tim Harrington called for the execution of the leaders, with the clear backing of William Martin Murphy, the owner of the paper. By November 1921, Murphy Senior had died and his place as chairman had been taken by his son, William Lombard Murphy.

The *Freeman's Journal* was unequivocal in its reaction to the events in Croke Park, which a headline on page five proclaimed was 'Amritzar Repeated in Dublin', referring to the massacre at Jallianwala Bagh in Amritzar in India, which had taken place in April 1919. Acting Brigadier-General Reginald Dyer had ordered troops of the British Indian Army to fire on unarmed civilians at a banned meeting, resulting in an estimated 379 dead and 1,200 wounded. The *Freeman's Journal* accused the Auxiliaries of carrying out reprisals on innocent civilians, without even the excuse that the crowd at Croke Park was doing anything illegal. The editorial in the *Freeman's Journal* of 22 November asked:

'*WHERE WILL IT END?*
In the morning some fourteen officers and men of the Military and Secret Services were shot dead, at the same hour, in widely separated districts of the city – some in hotels, some in private residences.

In the afternoon the authorised answer of the Government agents came in the form of an attack upon a football crowd assembled, unsuspecting of evil, to watch a match in Croke Park.

Croke Park was turned into Amritzar with the difference that there were no proclamations, no warnings, no legalities defied by the assembly in Croke Park.

The slaughter was a classic example of a Government reprisal.

The innocent were shot down in blind vengeance.

The pretence that the firing was provoked by an attack upon the Government forces will decieve no one in Ireland. It is another base official lie.'

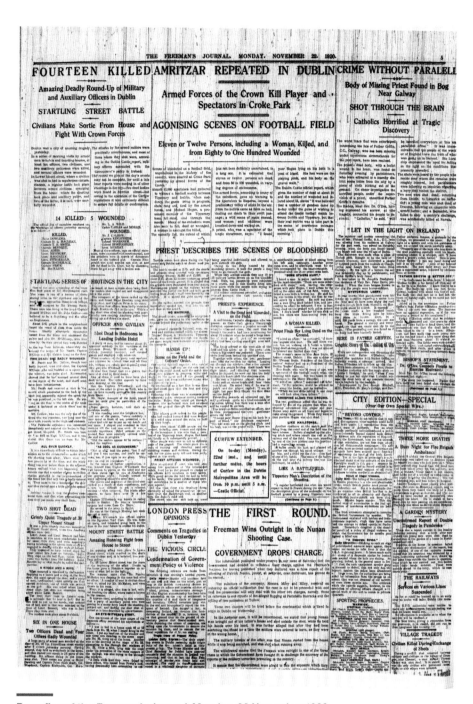

Page five of the *Freeman's Journal*, Monday, 22 November 1920.
(Courtesy of Dublin City Library and Archive)

Most of the other Irish newspapers followed the *Irish Independent's* approach in trying to maintain a balance in their coverage of the two sets of killings. The DORA regulations empowered the British forces to shut down any paper that was too obviously sympathetic to the separatist cause. Over 35 newspapers had been suppressed, with equipment removed from their offices, between 1919 and 1920. The *Cork Examiner* was closed for the crime of publishing an advertisement for the Dáil loan, which was already in wide circulation. Newspapers became embroiled in expensive court appeals against the restrictions on them.

The *Irish Times* was firmly unionist in its approach and was adamant that His Majesty's Forces were murdered and wounded in their houses in the morning while the afternoon's casualties were caused by "Wild Scenes at Gaelic Football Match". In a short report on 22 November the story repeated Dublin Castle's version of events, with no analysis of the official statement:

> *'Yesterday morning there was enacted in Dublin a series of crimes unparalleled in the history of the city. As a result, fourteen members of His Majesty's Forces were murdered in their houses, and a number of others seriously wounded.*
>
> *Later in the day, while a Gaelic football match was being played at Croke Park, Jones's Road, where many thousands of people were assembled, Forces of the Crown arrived, with the object of searching for perpetrators of the crimes of the morning. According to the official report, these forces were instantly fired on by pickets of civilians guarding the grounds, and the Crown Forces immediately replied.*
>
> *The result of this action was a violent stampede amongst the spectators and more firing, in the course of which it is estimated that ten persons were killed and upwards of fifty wounded. In addition to those wounded by gunfire, many suffered from injuries received in the stampede.'*

A further story, headed 'Statements by Onlookers', similarly contained no analysis of the stories told by people the reporter met who were escaping from the stadium. This testimony made it clear that the lorries and armoured cars carrying the armed forces were very organised and surrounded Croke Park before the firing began. Following a listing of the casualties and the nature of their injuries, there was a very vague summary of what was claimed to have happened:

> *'It is stated that scouts were posted around the field, and that when the military arrived they were fired upon and returned the fire. In the rush which followed a woman was crushed to death. Thirty revolvers, it is said, were found in the football ground after the visit of the armed forces.'*

BELFAST NEWS-LETTER, MOND

DAY OF APPALLING TRAGEDIES

Twenty-four Killed in Dublin.

COURTS-MARTIAL OFFICERS MURDERED.

Scenes of Carnage at Gaelic Football Match.

Dublin yesterday was the scene of an unprecedented outbreak of organised crime, resulting in the murders of twelve Army officers and ex-officers associated with the bringing to justice of Sinn Fein gunmen. In addition two members of the auxiliary police were shot dead.

In the cases of the officers and ex-officers the victims were killed in bed or in rooms in the hotels and lodgings at which they had been residing. Four of the assassins were captured, including one who was wounded.

Later in the day forces of the Crown proceeding to the venue of a Gaelic football match, to effect arrests, were fired on by a Sinn Fein

CROKE PARK AFFAIR.

10 KILLED: 50 WOUNDED.

Search for Gunmen Leads to Resistance.

CROWN FORCES REPLY TO FIRE.

The following official report was issued last night:—

It is believed that a number of gunmen came to Dublin ostensibly to attend the Gaelic football match between Dublin and Tipperary at Croke Park, but that their real motive was to take part in the series of murderous outrages which took place in Dublin on Sunday morning. In this belief it was decided to make investigations at the match itself, and for this purpose a mixed party of military, R.I.C., and auxiliary police were detailed. They approached tho grounds at Croke Park from different directions, and found that pickets had been posted at the various approaches to the field to give warning, presumably, on the arrival of the forces of the Crown. These pickets not only raised the alarm, but also fired on the approaching troops. The firing was returned, and a number of casualties were sustained by people who were watching the

Page six of *Belfast News-Letter,* Monday 22 November 1920.
(Courtesy of Irish Newspaper Archives, available in all Dublin City Libraries)

Not surprisingly, the unionist *Belfast News-Letter* also quoted the official statement from Dublin Castle as the definitive account. The headline on the version of the events in the afternoon is 'Croke Park Affair' and the sub-headings essentially call the innocence of the crowd into question. Responsibility for the 'Scenes of Carnage' referred to in the longer story about the 'Day of Appalling Tragedies' is laid firmly at the door of Sinn Féin gunmen.

Sinn Féin politicians were fully aware of the need to maintain a strong relationship with the Irish press but they also felt the need to make the Irish case for independence internationally. The Dáil Propaganda Department produced the *Irish Bulletin*, which was a news sheet printed several times a week. It gained a reputation for accuracy, especially when compared to the official *Weekly Summary* issued by Dublin Castle, which was considered to be full of black propaganda. The *Bulletin's* first editor was Desmond Fitzgerald, who was the Dáil's Head of Propaganda, a title which was changed later to Head of Publicity, suggesting increased self-confidence in the Dáil's perception of its legitimacy as a government.

In the issue of the *Irish Bulletin* produced on 24 November 1920, the first to come out after Bloody Sunday, the headline pulled no punches and the report went on to dissect the official statements and prove their falsehood:

'THE IRISH AMRITZAR
TWO OFFICIAL REPORTS – AND THE TRUTH

Two official accounts were issued, explaining the Amritzar at Croke Park, Dublin on Sunday November 21st 1920. Both are false. Even if the evidence did not prove them to be false, they are themselves demonstrably so. The first official account was issued from Dublin Castle late on Sunday night. It contained the following passages:

> *"They (a mixed party of military, RIC and Auxiliary Police) approached the ground from different directions and found that pickets had been posted at the various approaches to the field to give warning, presumably, of the arrival of Forces of the Crown. These pickets not only raised the alarm but also fired on the approaching troops. The firing was returned and a number of casualties were sustained by people who were watching the match. In addition to the injuries sustained through this firing, several persons, it is believed, were badly crushed in the stampede which ensued."*

It will be noticed that this official report makes it quite clear that those killed and wounded were killed and wounded by the fire of troops and constabulary outside the field. It happens that Croke Park is surrounded by walls 20 feet high.

The *Bulletin* offered further explanation why the official report was false. It challenged Sir Hamar Greenwood, the Irish Chief Secretary, to explain the significant inconsistencies in the official statement and in the report he made to the House of Commons in Westminster. No such explanation was forthcoming, and Greenwood stood by his claims. In response to a question in the British House of Commons on 23 November, he replied:

> *'Events in the football ground went to show that this belief was well founded, and that a considerable number among the crowd were carrying arms. That was proved beyond doubt by their efforts to escape.'*

Obviously it did not occur to him that escaping from the grounds was the logical thing to do when armed men, who had arrived in armoured vehicles, were shooting into the crowd.

On Wednesday, 24 November, the *Irish Independent's* review of what the provincial press was saying about Bloody Sunday made it clear that nationalist papers at least were not accepting the official version of what happened in Croke Park, although they were also appalled at the assassination of the British officers by the Squad. The tone of the *Cork Examiner's* editorial was typical of others in its plea for peace:

Sir Hamar Greenwood, Chief Secretary for Ireland (Courtesy of *Illustrated London News*)

'The state of affairs has become so appalling that the necessity for the Truce advocated by his Grace the Archbishop of Tuam has become imperative and its urgency is great. The bloodshed that is taking place, and which claims military, civilians, and auxiliaries amongst its victims, is a calamity that must fill with horror the mind of every individual endowed with the instincts of humanity, who regards human life as sacred.'

The *Irish Independent's* review mentioned other references to Archbishop Kilmartin's truce proposal, and the fact that it was also being welcomed in England.

Belfast's *Irish News* reported on 22 November, in a fairly one-sided condemnation of the violence and referred only to the 'hundreds of crimes' against civilians that had been committed under the auspices of the British Government's 'Irish Policy':

'Bloodshed cannot be stopped by the sword; it will be ended when the right of Ireland to national liberty has been recognised – when the sword and the rotten governmental system upheld by the sword have been sheathed and cast down, and peace established on the enduring foundations of freedom and international good will.'

There was a consistent policy of suppressing Irish newspapers during the War of Independence, sometimes with violent attacks on personnel, as well as removal of equipment and closure of the papers' operations. The *Atlas of the Irish Revolution* contains a valuable map of suppressions and/or attacks, with data compiled by Ian Kenneally. The number of incidents, including 27 in Dublin, between the commencement of the war in January 1919 and the truce in July 1921, gives an indication of the extent of the censorship and the brutality of its implementation. The Crown forces were not the only bodies involved in attacks on newspapers, although they were certainly responsible for the majority of them. In his essay in the *Atlas,* Kenneally notes that the IRA also tried to silence sections of the press who were considered to be 'hampering the work of the Republic and weakening their position through the country by advocating a policy of moderation'.

In the weeks following Bloody Sunday, the Irish newspapers attempted to cover the investigations and how they were being conducted. On 24 November, the *Irish Independent* reported that the president of the military court had been instructed to hold a closed inquiry and adjourned the hearings pending further instruction. Only evidence of identity and medical testimony were taken in the case of the thirteen victims of the Croke Park shooting (the fourteenth victim would die on 26 November).

The *Irish Times* continued to accept Dublin Castle's statements on the events in Croke Park. The editorial of 23 November reported on the scene in the Westminster Parliament when Joseph Devlin was shouted down loudly by other MPs for asking a question of Hamar Greenwood about the casualties among the football crowd. The main thrust of the piece was to praise English forbearance in the face of 'Irish intractability'.

'For more than a generation the English people have been consistently well disposed to Ireland. They had been puzzled and disappointed by her refusal to reciprocate their friendship. They have wondered why, as the Prime Minister said in a recent speech, Ireland has been most disdainful and distrustful at the very moments when England was most ready to give substantial proofs of her goodwill. ... It has admitted, with almost extravagant humility, the crimes and blunders of Irish administrations in the past. Even the rampant disloyalty of the Republican movement and its intrigues with hostile Powers did not break the almost illimitable patience of the English people. ... The story of the brutal murder of fourteen servants of the Crown in their bedrooms has forced the sanest and most equable assembly in the world to "see red". Englishmen understand clean fighting; they can make allowances even for the lawless frenzy of the fanatic; but they cannot pardon or excuse the deliberate and wholesale assassination of defenceless men.'

Coverage of the events of Bloody Sunday continued to dominate the headlines for the next week or so until the ambush at Kilmichael in County Cork on 28 November took over. As in the case of Bloody Sunday, editorial policy was largely dictated by the political stance of the newspaper. The burning of Cork on 10 December was condemned widely, not least because it cast such doubt on David Lloyd George's claim that the Government had 'murder by the throat'.

It is understandable that Irish newspapers often self-censored during the War of Independence because the Defence of the Realm Act meant they could be suppressed completely if they were too open in their defiance of the military authorities. As with all wars it tends to be the civilians who suffer most and on 21 November 1920 the people who set out to watch a football match in Croke Park became part of that bloody toll.

Sketch of Gunmen. This *Illustrated London News* imagining of the Squad's attack on British officers would not have been out of place in certain British and Irish publications, in the aftermath of Bloody Sunday. (Courtesy of *Illustrated London News*)

Further Reading

- Ian Kenneally, *The Paper Wall. Newspapers and Propaganda in Ireland 1919-1921.* The Collins Press, 2008.

- Ian Kenneally, "Irish Newspapers during the War of Independence" in John Crowley, Donal Ó Drisceoil and Mike Murphy ; associate editor: John Borgonovo (Eds.), *Atlas of the Irish Revolution.* Cork University Press, 2017, pp. 385-389.

- Ian Kenneally, *"The Irish Bulletin"* in Atlas of the Irish Revolution, pp. 483-486.

- Aubane Historical Society, *Irish Bulletin : a full reprint of the official newspaper of Dáil Eireann giving news and war reports: Volume 1,12th July 1919 to 1st May 1920.* Cork, 2012.

- Irish Newspaper Archives at www.irishnewsarchive.com (can be consulted for free at Dublin City Library and Archive)

Dick McKee: 'A Famous Finglas Patriot'

James Curry, Historian in Residence, Dublin North West

2020 marks the centenary of the death of Dick McKee, a senior figure within the Irish Volunteers who was killed along with two other prisoners, Peadar Clancy and Conor Clune, while in custody at Dublin Castle during the War of Independence. This chapter provides an overview of McKee's life and discusses some of the public and private ways that the Irish revolutionary has been remembered in the century since his death.

Although it is traditionally believed that Richard 'Dick' McKee was born at his Phibsborough Road home in Dublin on 4 April 1893, a birth certificate missing his Christian name indicates that he was born on 6 April 1892 at the Rotunda Hospital.[1] McKee's father Patrick, who came from Kiltale in County Meath, was a market gardener, while his mother Bridget (née O'Leary) hailed from Fermoy in County Cork. They had five children together with Dick, the eldest, followed by Mary (Maire), Johanna, Margaret and Patrick. After several years spent in Rathdrum, County Dublin, the McKee family were recorded in the 1901 national census as living at Drumshanbo Town, County Leitrim, with the head of the household employed as a steward and domestic servant. Shortly afterwards, the family returned to Dublin, where Patrick McKee died from 'general paralysis' on 23 March 1906. His widow moved the family from 29 Royal Canal Bank to 2 Finglas Bridge Town, and the 1911 census shows Dick McKee employed as a 'paper warehouse assistant' and living in Finglas with his mother and younger brother Patrick.

McKee was educated at St. Paul's Christian Brothers School on North Brunswick Street, Smithfield ('The Brunner'). After passing the Junior Grade Intermediate examination, he was apprenticed to the well-known Dublin publishing house of M. H. Gill & Son Ltd., where in due course he became a compositor (person who sets the type/text for printing). A keen sportsman, McKee was fond of cycling and a fine handball player. Over six feet tall and broad-shouldered, he joined the Irish Volunteers in 1913 and enlisted as a member of 'G'. Company, 2nd Battalion, Dublin Brigade. A natural leader, he was soon placed in charge of this company. During the 1916 Easter Rising, McKee served as a captain under Commandant Thomas McDonagh at Jacob's Biscuit Factory. After the Rising, he was incarcerated in Knutsford Jail in England and Frongoch Camp in North Wales until August 1916.

Once back in Ireland, McKee rose rapidly through the ranks of the Irish Volunteers and was promoted to commandant of the Dublin Brigade's 2nd Battalion. He was also appointed to the general headquarters staff of the Irish Volunteers as Director of Training. In March 1918 McKee became officer commanding of the Dublin Brigade. Before taking up this position, however, he was arrested on St. Patrick's Day while training his battalion at field work in north County Dublin and sentenced to three months imprisonment at Mountjoy Prison and Dundalk. Upon release, McKee took command of the Dublin Brigade and was responsible for most of its operations during this period, including a raid on Collinstown Aerodrome in March 1919, planning the escape of Piaras Béaslaí and J. J. Walsh from Mountjoy Prison in October 1919, and efforts to assassinate the Lord Lieutenant of Ireland, John French.

Photograph of a youthful Dick McKee
(Courtesy of Military Archives, BMH P 13-001,
Bureau of Military History Photographs collection)

In November 1919 McKee was captured during a raid on the Harcourt Street offices of Dáil Éireann and once more sentenced to three months imprisonment. Upon release in January 1920, he resigned from his job to focus solely on Irish Volunteer activities, entering what would prove to be the final phase of his life. His younger sister Maire took up employment at M. H. Gill & Son Ltd. following his departure from the firm. Having narrowly escaped arrest the previous month, McKee was captured on 20 November 1920 at a Gloucester Street (now Sean McDermott Street) safe house along with Peadar Clancy, vice-commandant of the Dublin Brigade, shortly after the pair had left Parnell Square's Vaughan's Hotel due to a raid. 'Bloody Sunday' took place the following day. Hours before the Croke Park shootings, IRA gunmen had spread out across Dublin and killed British officers whom they suspected of being spies and informers. McKee was closely involved in the preparations for these shootings.

Dick McKee, Seán Fitzpatrick and Peadar Clancy
(Courtesy of the National Library of Ireland)

When the *Weekly Irish Times* appeared six days after Bloody Sunday, the front page was inevitably still taken up with the 'orgy of bloodshed' witnessed at Croke Park. The paper published Dublin Castle's official report which insisted that the soldiers and police had only opened fire inside the stadium after they were fired upon first. Less prominence was given to the previous weekend's fatal shooting at Dublin Castle of Dick McKee, Peadar Clancy, and a Gaelic League enthusiast and apparent intelligence officer with the IRA from County Clare named Conor Clune (who had been arrested at Vaughan's Hotel on 20 November).[2] According to Dublin Castle's report, which deserves to be quoted in full:

> 'At about 11 o'clock on Monday Richard McKee, T.C. Clune, and Peter Clancy were killed in an attempt to escape from the old Detective Office, Exchange Court, Dublin, where they were in police custody. These men were arrested on Saturday night, but owing to lack of prison accommodation were detained in a guardroom adjoining the entrance which they shared with a guard of four men. The room contains a large quantity of army material and equipment – mattresses in piles,

beds, a table and bench, rifles, ammunition, etc. The prisoners were allowed considerable freedom of movement and were seated round the fire at the moment of their attempted escape. The guard on duty had his back to them while the two men who were off duty were sitting reading. The commander of the guard was in the doorway of the passage. Most of the garrison at the building were out on duty, and this must have been evident to the prisoners, as the only exit from the building is through this room.

The three prisoners suddenly rose to their feet and the sentry turned round on hearing the noise. One of the prisoners had a Mills' bomb in his hand which he had abstracted from a box of bombs under a bed. This he threw at the sentry. The bomb did not explode, because (unknown to the prisoner) none of the bombs had been detonated.

The sentry jumped to one side and the prisoner, throwing a second bomb, dashed behind a pile of mattresses when the sentry fired. Another of the prisoners, meanwhile had seized a rifle and fired at the other members of the guard. Both ducked behind the table, which was upset, and the shot lodged in the wall.

The third prisoner lifted a shovel lying near the fire and aimed a blow at the men who were crouching behind the overturned table. The shovel crashed into the wood, but missed the men. The commander of the guard hearing the firing at this moment rushed into the room and fired.

This sudden diversion enabled both his companions to rise from the table, and firing together the second and third prisoner fell simultaneously.

The whole affair lasted only a few seconds. It is presumed that the prisoners, who had seen all the movements of the garrison since Saturday night had observed that at 11 o'clock most of the men were out on duty and that they were practically alone in the building with the guard of four men.'

This written account was reinforced and supported with the release of photographs by Dublin Castle reconstructing what was claimed to have happened. But instead of succeeding, these staged images only made members of the Irish public even more suspicious. Within a week, Dáil Éireann's *Irish Bulletin* was reporting that the three prisoners had been tortured and murdered by Auxiliary members of the Royal Irish Constabulary as a 'reprisal' attack for the British casualties suffered on the morning of Bloody Sunday. McKee's sister Maire claimed that her brother had been stabbed as well as shot. Another witness alleged that McKee's ribs were broken, and that his torso had been ripped to shreds with bayonets.

One of the photographs released by Dublin Castle after the deaths of Dick McKee, Peadar Clancy and Conor Clune, reconstructing the alleged 'attempt to escape' which led to the killing of the three men (Courtesy of Mercier Archive)

Officially, McKee's death certificate states that he was killed on Monday 22 November, while attempting to escape from Dublin Castle. His cause of death was registered as 'shock and haemorrhage due to bullet wounds fired by members of the auxiliary division [of] R.I.C. in self-defence and in execution of their duty, i.e. in preventing the escape of the deceased who was in their lawful custody'. This information was 'received from [a] military court of inquiry – held at King George V Hospital, city of Dublin'. The loss of its commanding officer and vice commandant was a crippling blow to the Dublin Brigade of the Irish Volunteers. McKee and Clancy were buried in Glasnevin Cemetery, with a large procession marching from the Pro-Cathedral on Marlborough Street. The fact

When the Black and Tans were Here.

And their Murder Gang butchered

DICK McKEE and PEADAR CLANCY

They did not say to them:

"In Fundamentals and in Ideals we are the same."

It was left to General Mulcahy to say things like this 48 hours after his Murder Gang had, in cold blood butchered Sean Cole, Alf Colley, and Bernard Daly because they refused to be dragged into the British Empire.

Irish Civil War flyer referencing the deaths of Dick McKee and Peadar Clancy (Courtesy of Dublin City Library and Archive)

that so many IRA figures attended the funeral and risked arrest, including Michael Collins, shows the esteem in which both men were held. Collins, who ensured that both men were buried in military uniform, was devastated at the loss of his 'good friends', whom he described in a memorial wreath message as 'two of Ireland's best soldiers'. Conor Clune's remains were taken back to County Clare and buried at Quin Abbey.

The loss of its primary wage earner left the McKee family in precarious circumstances, leading the Irish Free State to repeatedly provide financial assistance over the coming years. On 4 January 1923, McKee's mother Bridget wrote the following letter to Adjutant General Gearóid O'Sullivan at Portobello Barracks:

> 'Over a year ago I made a claim verbally for Dick's motorcycle which was taken in a raid; and at the time inquiries were made in Dublin Castle. I was given to understand, then, that I would get the machine or its value. There were two taken, one personal property, the other army property. I don't know whether this matter lapsed altogether or was forgotten, not having heard any more about it.
>
> I decided at the time that I would take the value of the [motor] cycle and as I have pressing need of the money at the moment I should be glad if you could settle the matter now.'

Eight days later, O'Sullivan sent the following typed memo to Richard Mulcahy, the Minister for Defence:

> 'I spoke to you about a letter I had from Mrs. McKee. You remember I was speaking to you about the raid on Dick McKee's bicycle, and you more or less agreed that we should see that compensation was granted. I now attach a letter from Mrs. McKee. Could anything be done?'

Bridget McKee's request was, unsurprisingly, granted. Mulcahy was able to report on 30 January that at an Executive Council meeting of the Irish Free State Government:

> '... it was mentioned that application had been made by the mother of the late Richard McKee for compensation in respect of her son's motorcycle valued at £50 which had been seized by the British Military. In view of the fact that Mrs. McKee is urgently in need of money, payment of £50 by way of a loan out of the [Dáil Éireann] Special Fund ... was approved.'

At the time, an 'urgent' letter had been sent to the acting Minister for Finance, W. T. Cosgrave from the Irish Army's Commander-in-Chief, which stated that:

> 'Dick McKee was Commandant of the Dublin Brigade and one of the most important members of the G. H. Q. Staff at the time of his death. His mother who is financially embarrassed at present, asks for compensation in respect of a motor bicycle of his that was taken by the British. It is the wish of the Cabinet that a payment of £50 be made to her from the special fund and in respect of the motor bicycle in question.'

On 3 February, one month after her request, Bridget McKee received a cheque for £50 from Government Buildings.

A couple of months later, W. T. Cosgrave, in his position as the President of the Executive Council of the Irish Free State, reported at a meeting of his Cabinet, 'that he had received ... an application for funds for the relief of the family of the late Richard McKee who had lost his life in the Anglo-Irish struggle. One of the sisters was in very delicate health and had been ordered abroad by the doctor'. The result of this application was that another grant was issued from Dáil Éireann's 'Special Fund', this time for a sum of £100. Six days later, Bridget McKee acknowledged the cheque, noting that the money would be used to allow her daughter Maire to travel 'abroad for her health'.

More financial assistance was to be provided to the McKee family. At an Executive Council meeting held on 11 May, a decision was made to award Bridget McKee a further £150. The following year, she was then awarded £1,200 by the Department of Defence's Compensation (Personal Injuries) Committee. In 1954 Maire McKee was awarded an annual dependant's allowance of £125.

These financial grants were evidence that Dick McKee had not been forgotten by those in power after the founding of the Irish Free State. And in subsequent years, the Finglas resident was remembered in more public ways, including a memorial tablet at Dublin Castle commemorating Peadar Clancy, Conor Clune and McKee for giving 'their lives for the cause of Irish independence'. This was erected in 1939 by the National Graves Association.

On 1 March 1951 a bronze bust of McKee was unveiled inside the officers' mess room at McKee Barracks on Blackhorse Avenue in Dublin (formerly Marlborough Barracks) by the Minister for Defence, Dr. Thomas F. O'Higgins, who was reported as saying how proud he was 'to have the privilege of unveiling a bust to commemorate the memory of one of the grandest characters and one of the greatest soldiers who had ever decorated the glorious pages of Ireland's history'. O'Higgins went on to state that McKee's death 'should never be regarded by anyone as a life sacrificed in vain ... It was one of the milestones up that hard road to ultimate success [and] victory'. The bust by sculptor Laurence Campbell was paid for out of money raised by officers at the barracks who felt that it 'should have a suitable memorial of the man after whom it was named', and cast in bronze by a Finglas company, Parlanti Ireland Ltd.

A 1971 photograph of Finglas village with the Dick McKee Memorial Monument visible on the far left. (Courtesy of Dublin City Library and Archive)

Shortly afterwards came another honour closer to home. In January 1951 the *Irish Press* announced that later in the year, on a site provided by Dublin Corporation, a monument was to be 'erected in the village of Finglas, Co. Dublin, to a famous Finglas patriot, Brigadier Dick McKee, who was killed by British Forces in Dublin Castle'. On 10 June, this fifteen-foot memorial was unveiled by Éamon de Valera. Along with the founding of a Dick McKee Memorial Pipe Band and annual commemorative events, the naming of a handful of roads and avenues in Finglas after McKee, Clancy and Clune also showed a local determination to ensure that what took place at Dublin Castle's guardroom in November 1920 was never forgotten.

At the conclusion of the official unveiling by Éamon de Valera on 10 June 1951, the Dick McKee Memorial Monument is blessed by local parish priest Father Ernest Farrell. Standing to de Valera's left is Andrew Darcy, President of Finglas's Dick McKee Memorial Pipe Band. The tall man behind de Valera is Fianna Fáil TD Patrick Joseph Burke. (Courtesy of Pauline O'Leary)

Dick McKee was described by *An t-Óglách,* an army publication he contributed to as well as set up and printed not long before his death, as 'the life and soul of [Irish] Volunteer operations, not merely in Dublin but in other parts of Ireland'. On 31 March 1954 he was posthumously awarded a 1916 Medal and Service Medal (1917-1921) with Bar by the Department of Defence.

McKee Avenue, Finglas in 1969
(Courtesy of Dublin City Library and Archive)

A 1948 photograph of the Finglas-based Dick McKee Memorial Pipe Band
(Courtesy of Pauline O'Leary)

Further Reading

- Andrews, C. S. *Dublin Made Me: An Autobiography.* Mercier, 1979.

- Brown, Kevin John. *They Died on Bloody Sunday.* Quin Memorial Committee, 1971.

- Coleman, Marie. *'McKee, Dick (Richard)'. Dictionary of Irish Biography.*

- Daly, Ronnie & O'Brien, Paul. *McKee Barracks. A Concise History.* Defence Forces Printing Press, 2018.

- Dempsey, Pauric J. *'Clancy, Peadar'. Dictionary of Irish Biography.*

- Forester, Margery. *Michael Collins: The Lost Leader.* Gill & MacMillan, 1989.

- O'Mahony, Sean. *Three Murders in Dublin Castle, 1920.* Elo Publications, 2000.

- Valiulis, Maryann Gialanella. *Portrait of a revolutionary: General Richard Mulcahy and the founding of the Irish Free State.* University Press of Kentucky, 1992.

- *Irish Bulletin*

- *An tÓglách*

- Bureau of Military History Witness Statements and Military Service Pensions Collection, Military Archives.

1 The fact that his sister Mary (Maire) was born on 8 December 1893 supports the suggestion that Dick McKee was born in April 1892 rather than April 1893, along with the fact that he was listed as nine and nineteen years old in the 1901 and 1911 national censuses.

2 Material contained in a successful application for a Military Service Pension made on her brother's behalf in the 1950s by Margaret T. Clune, suggests that as well as his Gaelic League activities, Conor Clune had been a member of the IRA for several years before his death, serving as an intelligence officer with the 4th Battalion of the East Clare Brigade or a Tuamgraney Company attached to that Battalion. As well as awarding the unmarried Margaret T. Clune a partial dependant's allowance on his behalf, the State also posthumously awarded Conor Clune a Service (1917-1921) Medal with Bar for his military service.

After Bloody Sunday... Murders, Raids and Roundups

Catherine Scuffil, Historian in Residence, Dublin South Central and South East

Tensions in Ireland were building throughout the month of November 1920. The Royal Irish Constabulary (RIC) in the country areas and the Dublin Metropolitan Police (DMP) in Dublin city, usually supported by the military, carried out numerous raids, with fairs and markets the principal targets in rural areas. Business premises, suspected of connections to Sinn Féin, and many private homes were also raided by the Crown forces. Fifty different private houses were raided in a single day, 6 November 1920, with household members detained in many cases.

These events led up to what became known as 'Bloody Sunday', 21 November 1920, a day of serious violence in Dublin with 32 men/boys and a woman killed or fatally wounded in various incidents throughout the day. The day started with the IRA, under Michael Collins, seeking out undercover British intelligence agents, known as the 'Cairo Gang', with 15 people killed or fatally wounded. In the afternoon, during a GAA Gaelic football match between Dublin and Tipperary in Croke Park, Auxiliaries and RIC members fired on the crowd, killing or fatally wounding fourteen, some estimates put the wounded at up to sixty people. The day ended when three Irish republican suspects, Dick McKee, Peadar Clancy and Conor Clune, were beaten and killed whilst in custody in Dublin Castle as they were 'trying to escape'.

However, the carnage and consequences associated with Bloody Sunday did not end there. Subsequent days and months saw further murders, reprisals, raids and a general roundup of prisoners as the British authorities tried to regain control of Ireland.

One casualty of Bloody Sunday was Joseph (Joe) Traynor, aged twenty-one, from Ballymount, County Dublin. Joe was born in Drimnagh Castle in 1900 and throughout his short life lived in different locations in the then rural areas of Inchicore, Drimnagh and the general district of Fox and Geese. A keen sportsman,

Joe was captain of Young Emmets GAA club's Gaelic football team on the Naas Road. Like many in the area he was also a member of the Irish Volunteers, serving with 'F' Company, 4th Battalion, Dublin Brigade.

As gunfire rang out in Croke Park, Joe, who was at the match with some friends and located at the canal end of the stadium, was shot twice in the back as he tried to escape over the wall. Although severely injured, he managed to make his way along a pathway near the railway track, where he was found by members of the Ring family, residents in nearby Sackville Gardens. They gave first-aid and assistance to the badly injured man in the kitchen of their home, but quickly realising that Joe needed immediate hospital treatment, they carried him through their house to the back lane near Ballybough Road. From here, Joe was collected by ambulance and brought to Jervis Street Hospital where he later died. Joe's good friend P.J. Ryan, who had accompanied him to the match, brought the tragic news to Joe's parents in their Ballymount cottage that their son had been caught up in the events in Croke Park and had been taken to hospital. Later that day a policeman officially informed them of the news that Joe had died.

**Joseph Traynor in his
Young Emmets GAA gear**
(Courtesy of Micheál Nelson)

After Bloody Sunday, an intensive campaign of arrest and general roundup of anyone with IRA associations began. Ballykinlar, County Down was the first internment camp set up, followed by others in Bere and Spike Islands in Cork, and the Curragh Camp in County Kildare. On Monday 22 November 1920, brothers Liam, Patrick and Christopher Ring were arrested at their home in Sackville Gardens as part of this roundup. They were each given a twelve month sentence of detention and were among the first internees at Ballykinlar. The reprisal for the Ring family was not unexpected, as all five sons had fought in the 1916 Easter Rising.

Another family with 1916 connections were also to suffer as a result of Bloody Sunday. The Doyle's were a well-regarded local family in Dolphin's Barn, near the South Circular Road, Dublin. Having lived for a number of years at Emerald Terrace - a group of nine small houses just off Cork Street - the family of nine, mother Margaret, father Thomas Snr. and his brother John, four daughters and two sons, moved to a larger house at 3 Dolphin's Barn Street. This house backed onto the premises of the Mirror Laundry and was directly opposite Emerald Square, where during the 1916 Rising, Éamonn Ceannt and his men had mobilised before heading for the South Dublin Union and Marrowbone Lane Distillery.

The new location suited the Doyle family well as Thomas Snr. and John both worked in Roe's Distillery on Thomas Street. Four of the Doyle children worked in the nearby City Woollen Mills, where one son, Thomas Jnr. was a loom-tuner and engine man. Thomas Jnr. had been a member of Fianna Éireann (the youth wing of the nationalist movement) from 1910 to 1917 and served with the Irish Volunteers/IRA from 1917. Some sources suggest that he had fought during the 1916 Easter Rising at Jameson's Distillery, Marrowbone Lane. His older brother, Christopher, was a member of 'C' Company 4th Battalion, Dublin Brigade of the Irish Volunteers.

On Monday 22 November 1920, in what was regarded as a direct reprisal for the events of Bloody Sunday, the Doyle home was raided by a group of Auxiliaries. Thomas Jnr. had just returned from his job and was washing himself in the yard at the rear of the house. Some of the raiding party entered the yard, and seeing him, fired at him with fatal results. His mother Margaret and some of his sisters were present at the time. The deceased was brought to the Meath Hospital. A Court of Inquiry was held in lieu of an inquest on 29 November 1920 at which his death certificate was issued. It stated that Thomas Jnr. had died almost immediately from shock and haemorrhage caused by bullet wounds.

Auxiliaries are briefed by an officer in Dublin Castle. This photograph was taken surreptitiously and used by the IRA to target and kill members of the Crown forces, whoever took it put their life at risk. (Courtesy of Dublin City Library and Archive)

Numerous raids were carried out on private houses in the Dublin area throughout the month of November 1920. One such raid took place at 4 St. Michael's Terrace, Blackpitts, a quiet cul-de-sac within the Belville estate in the city's Liberties area. This was the home of the Scuffil family; father Albert, aged fifty-two, was a house decorator and signwriter, as was his son Albert Jnr., aged twenty-one. Both men shared a mutual interest in racing pigeons. At 6.30am, on 6 November 1920, the quietness of the estate was disturbed by the arrival from Wellington Barracks (later Griffith Barracks, now the site of Griffith College) of two large military motor lorries, containing one officer and sixteen other ranks from the 1st Battalion Prince of Wales Volunteers, South Lancashire Regiment and a DMP officer. They sealed off the cul-de-sac and the officer in charge, Lieutenant H.E. Royes forced entry to the house. Inside he found Albert Snr. in bed, who was immediately arrested as was his son. Both men were taken to Wellington Barracks. In addition, the military took some letters and photographs, a pigeon permit, a book of pigeon notes and fifty pigeons! The two men were released without charge the following day when it was established that Albert Snr. kept his homing pigeons 'under permit from the English Government'. It was later revealed that the military were acting on information from Lieutenant Hodson of the 25th Brigade Intelligence Office. The events were widely reported in the newspapers and also mentioned in the *Irish Bulletin*, the official newspaper of Dáil

Éireann. The raid on the Scuffil home was just one of a number of raids carried out that day including the drapery stores of T.J. Lemass at 2 Capel Street (future Taoiseach Seán Lemass' father's business) and Vaughan's Hotel on Parnell Square.

PIGEONS ARRESTED

About 6 o'clock this morning 4 St. Michael's Terrace, Blackpitts, was raided, and Mr Albert Scuffil and his son, aged 21 years, arrested.

Mr Scuffil is a well-known breeder of racing pigeons and has a licence or permit to keep the birds.

The raiders not only paid attention to Mr Scuffil and his son, but also to the pigeons, twelve of which were taken away. There were fifty pigeons altogether, and the raiders were understood to intimate that they would call again for the remainder.'

Report of the raid on the Scuffil house, Irish Examiner, 8 November 1920 (Courtesy of Irish Newspaper Archives, available in all Dublin City Libraries)

The *Irish Bulletin* also reported on private homes raided at Longwood Avenue and St. Theresa's Villas on the South Circular Road on 29 November 1920. This was a high-profile raid, as one of the houses targeted was that of Tom Kelly, the well-known alderman and city councillor. Whilst the Auxiliaries commented that they were looking for a Michael Kelly, when they called to the house they arrested Isaac, the eldest son of the alderman. Isaac was subsequently interned in Ballykinlar early in 1921. In June of that year, the *New Ross Standard* referenced an article that had been earlier carried by the *Roscommon Herald* headlined 'Romantic Marriage'. This reported on a wedding that had taken place in Ballykinlar camp between a Ms. Kathleen King of Carrick, near Mullingar, County Westmeath and the aforementioned Isaac Kelly, with the prison censor acting as witness on the occasion. The wedding ring was handmade in the camp from a hammered-out coin. The couple later had one daughter, named Kathleen for her mother. Katie Óg, as she was known, was the only grandchild of Alderman Tom Kelly to carry the family surname.

Alderman Tom Kelly
(Courtesy of Dublin City
Library and Archive)

The events of Bloody Sunday affected many people in the weeks and months that followed. Raids and reprisals meant further disruption, damage to household property, arrests and casualties, in some cases with fatal results. The impact of this was felt through the generations that followed.

People gather outside Jervis Street Hospital where the military inquiry into the Bloody Sunday killings took place (Courtesy of National Library of Ireland)

Alderman Kelly lost his brother David in March 1921. David Kelly was manager of the Sinn Féin Bank and was shot dead beside his home at 132 Great Brunswick Street (now Pearse Street) during a street battle between Auxiliaries and other armed men. His death notice ended with the comment *'His life for Ireland'*. The family suffered another tragedy in October 1932 when Isaac died unexpectedly at thirty-six years of age.

Albert Scuffil Snr. and his son Albert, continued to reside in 4 St. Michael's Terrace, Blackpitts and were well-known painters, decorators and sign-writers in the area, with the father specialising in church decoration. Following the events of 1920, the older Albert's interest in animal sports changed from breeding homing pigeons to racing greyhounds, with some measure of success over the years, especially at Harold's Cross stadium. When his son Albert married, he moved into a house across the road from his father. Albert Jnr. was my grandfather and family members still live in number 4 St. Michael's Terrace, which has witnessed the lives of six generations of the same family.

Thomas Doyle's parents received an ex-gratia payment of £50 granted by the Irish Free State in October 1924. A further special payment of £25 was made to his widowed mother in the 1930s, by which time his brother Christopher was living in Inchicore and serving as a detective with An Garda Síochána. No trace remains today of the Doyle family home in Dolphin's Barn Street - the houses and businesses at that location were demolished to make way for the 'new' Coombe Hospital in the late 1960s and later for road widening in the early 1990s. The mortuary of The Coombe University Hospital is located almost on the site of the yard of the Doyle home where Thomas Jnr. was killed.

The house at number 5 Sackville Gardens remained with the Ring family until 1955 when it was bought by the Gregory family. The son, Tony Gregory TD lived here until his death in 2009. Speaking about the events of Bloody Sunday on the 99th anniversary, and particularly looking to the sad death of Joe Traynor, former Lord Mayor of Dublin, Nial Ring said, *'there still remains a unique, if sad, bond between our families'*. Nial is a direct descendant of the Ring brothers.

Following representations by Councillor Ring and others on Dublin City Council, the area beside Sackville Gardens from where Joe was removed by ambulance to Jervis Street Hospital on Bloody Sunday, is due to be renamed *Joseph Traynor Way* as a centenary tribute to him.

Thanks to Micheál Nelson, Orla Murphy, Liz Gillis, Councillor Nial Ring and the extended Scuffil family for permission to use and for general access to their private research.

Further Reading

- Carden, Sheila. *The Alderman - Alderman Tom Kelly (1868-1942)*. Dublin City Council, 2007.

- Nelson, Micheál. *Once Upon a Sunday, the story of Joseph P. Traynor (1900-1920)*. Personal/Family Publication.

- Gallagher, Mary. *16 Lives Éamonn Ceannt*. O'Brien Press, 2014.

- *Irish Bulletin*

- Bureau of Military History and Military Service Pensions Collection, Military Archives.

- British military records accessed through www.FindMyPast.ie, August 2020